A VISIT TO

Brazil

REVISED AND UPDATED

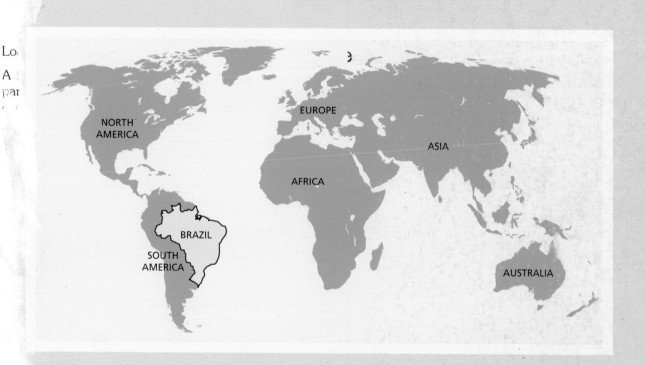

Peter and Connie Roop

Heinemann
LIBRARY

www.heinemann.co.uk/library
Visit our website to find out more information about Heinemann Library books.

To order:
☎ Phone 44 (0) 1865 888066
Send a fax to 44 (0) 1865 314091
Visit the Heinemann Bookshop at www.heinemann.co.uk/library to browse our catalogue and order online.

First published in Great Britain by Heinemann Library, Halley Court, Jordan Hill, Oxford OX2 8EJ, part of Pearson Education. Heinemann is a registered trademark of Pearson Education Ltd.

© Pearson Education Ltd 1998, 2008

Editorial: Sarah Shannon
Design: Joanna Hinton-Malivoire
Picture research: Mica Brancic
Production: Duncan Gilbert

Originated by Modern Age
Printed and bound in China by South China Printing Co. Ltd

ISBN 978 0 431 087252 (hardback)
12 11 10 09 08
10 9 8 7 6 5 4 3 2 1

ISBN 978 0 431 087399 (paperback)
12 11 10 09 08
10 9 8 7 6 5 4 3 2 1

British Library Cataloguing in Publication Data
Roop, Peter
A visit to Brazil. - New ed.
1. Brazil – Social conditions – 1985 – Juvenile literature
2. Brazil – Geography – Juvenile literature
3. Brazil – Social life and customs – 21th century – Juvenile literature
I.Title II.Roop, Connie III. Brazil
981'.065

Acknowledgements
The publishers would like to thank the following for permission to reproduce photographs: ©Alamy p. **18** (David R. Frazier Photolibrary, Inc.); ©Corbis p. **7** (Brooks Kraft); ©Getty Images p. **15**, **28**; ©Hutchison Library p. **23**, p.**12** (Errington), p. **9** (J Horner), p. **22** (C Macarthy), p. **5** (J von Puttkamer); ©Lonley Planet p. **21** (John Maier Jr); ©LUPE CUNHA pp. **20**, **26**; ©South American Pictures pp. **6**, **14**, **19**, **29**; ©Tony Morrison pp. **10**, **11**, **13**, **16**, **17**, **25**, **27**; ©Trip p. **24** (S Grant); ©ZEFA p. **8** (J Ramid).

Cover photograph of Rio de Janeiro, city with beach reproduced with permission of Getty Images (Taxi).

Our thanks to Nick Lapthorn and Clare Lewis for their comments in the preparation of this book.

Every effort has been made to contact copyright holders of any material reproduced in this book. Any omissions will be rectified in subsequent printings if notice is given to the publishers.

Contents

Any words appearing in bold, **like this**, are explained in the Glossary.

Brazil

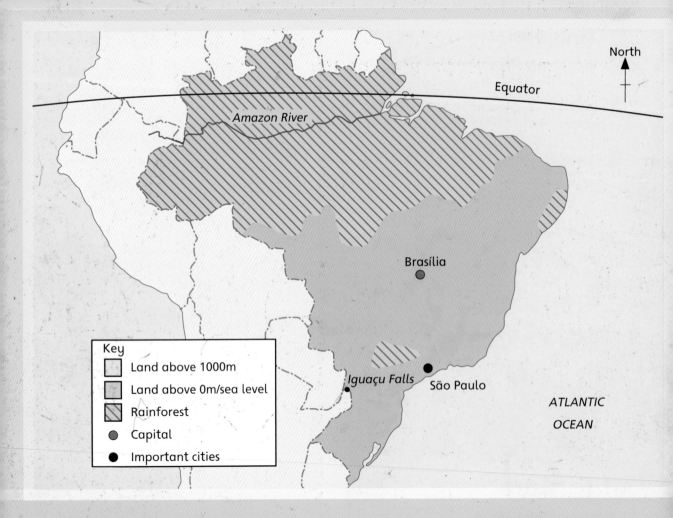

North

Equator

Amazon River

Brasília

Iguaçu Falls   São Paulo

ATLANTIC
OCEAN

Key
- ☐ Land above 1000m
- ▧ Land above 0m/sea level
- ▨ Rainforest
- ● Capital
- ● Important cities

Brazil is in South America. It is the fifth largest country in the world. The name Brazil comes from a tree which grows there and gives us Brazil nuts.

The first people in Brazil were **native people**. Then people from all over the world went to live in Brazil. They came from Europe, Africa and Asia.

Many native Brazilian people still live in the Amazon **rainforest**.

Brazil has **rainforests**, rivers, **grasslands** and beaches. Most of Brazil is south of the **equator**. Brazil has **tropical** weather.

Brazil has more people and land than any other country in South America. Most Brazilians live in or around the cities.

More than 10 million people live in the city of São Paulo.

Landmarks

The Amazon River flows through Brazil. It is the second longest river in the world. One thousand rivers run into the Amazon River.

8

The name Iguaçu comes from native words that mean "big water".

Iguaçu Falls is in Brazil. It is one of the most beautiful **waterfalls** in the world. It is on the **border** between Brazil and Argentina.

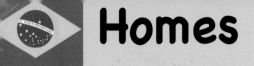

Homes

The people who live in São Paulo are called 'Paulistanos'.

Brasília is the **capital** city, but São Paulo is Brazil's largest city. It is one of the largest cities in the world.

Brazil has rich people but it has many more poor people. They live in **favelas** outside the big cities. Some Brazilians live in the rainforest.

Food

People have moved to Brazil from all around the world. They took with them many different **recipes**. Most recipes use rice, beef, pork, fruit, vegetables or beans.

Feijoada came from Africa and is the most popular food in Brazil. It is a stew of pork, beef, sausage, bacon and black beans. It is served with sliced oranges.

Clothes

Brazil has a **tropical climate**. It is usually warm so people wear light, cool clothing. **Native people** wear **traditional** clothes in the **rainforest**.

Dancers wear amazing costumes to perform in the carnival.

Brazilians have many **festivals** and holidays. This is when they like to dress up in colourful costumes.

Farmers in Brazil grow more sugar cane and coffee than almost any other country in the world. There are also lots of farmers or ranchers who have beef cattle.

16

There are many large iron mines, like this one, in Brazil.

Workers dig **iron ore** out of the ground to make steel. People in **factories** make steel, cloth, cars and other **products**. Brazil sells many of these products to other countries.

Transport

Brazilians travel by car, bus and truck. In the crowded cities some people share cars to save money and time.

People use boats to get about on the river.

The Amazon River is like a giant road into the centre of Brazil. People travel around the Amazon **Rainforest** by boat or by helicopter.

Languages

Portuguese is Brazil's national language. Explorers from Portugal took it to Brazil 500 years ago. Other Europeans travelled to Brazil too.

There are people from all over the world in Brazil today.

They took African **slaves** with them. Some people still speak African languages in Brazil. The first Brazilians were the **native people**. Their language is still spoken in Brazil today.

21

School

Most children go to school from the age of 7 to 17. They study many subjects including Portuguese, history, maths, science and art.

Many poor children work in street markets, or in **factories**.

Some Brazilian children are too poor to go to school. They must work to help feed their families.

Football (soccer) is called futebol.
It is the most popular sport in Brazil.
Most Brazilian children play futebol.

Capoeira is a Brazilian sport. It is like a fight, a dance and judo all in one. Other popular sports are basketball, volleyball, tennis and jogging.

Capoeira games often take place in a circle called a 'roda'.

Iemnajá is a Brazilian New Year's celebration. On New Year's Eve, people go to the beach. They give presents to Iemnajá, the goddess of the sea.

Thousands of people line the streets to watch the colourful parades.

Carnival is Brazil's biggest **festival**. It takes place about six weeks before Easter. There are **parades** through the noisy streets.

The Arts

Brazilians play music learned from the **native people**, Africans and from Europeans. People also like to play and sing choros or folk tunes.

The berimbau is a Brazilian **instrument**. It has one string and is played with a bow. Other popular instruments are guitars, banjos, drums and maracas.

Factfile

Name   The full name of Brazil is the Federative Republic of Brazil.

Capital   The capital city is Brasília.

Language   Most Brazilians speak Portuguese.

Population   There are 187 million people living in Brazil.

Money   Instead of the dollar or pound, Brazilians have the real.

Religions   Most Brazilians are Catholic or Protestant.

Products   Brazil produces more coffee and sugar cane than most other countries.

Words you can learn

olá   hello
tchau   goodbye
obrigato thank you
sim   yes
não   no
um   one
dois   two
três   three

Glossary

border where two countries meet

capital the city where the government is based

climate the normal type of weather for the area

equator an imaginary line around the earth dividing it into a northern half and a southern half

factories places where things are made

favelas large areas covered in small, roughly made huts where people live

festival a big celebration planned for lots of people to enjoy together

grasslands large flat areas where grasses are the only plants which grow

instrument something which makes music

iron ore the rock which contains iron

native people the first people who were living in Brazil

parade a group of people on show, dancing or walking together

products things which are grown, taken from the earth, made by hand or made in a factory

rainforest a thick forest that stays green all year and which has rain almost every day

recipe a set of directions for making food

slave a person who is taken from their home and family and sold to another person to do work

traditional the way something has been done or made for a long time

tropical hot and humid

waterfall where water falls down the side of a mountain

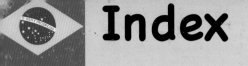

Index